MOVERS,
SHAKERS,
& HISTORY
MAKERS

LIL NAS X

RECORD-BREAKING MUSICIAN WHO BLURS THE LINES

CONTENT CONSULTANT
AARON X. SMITH, PhD
PROFESSOR OF AFRICAN AMERICAN STUDIES
TEMPLE UNIVERSITY

BY HENRIETTA TOTH

CAPSTONE PRESS
a capstone imprint

Capstone Captivate is published by Capstone Press, an imprint of Capstone.
1710 Roe Crest Drive
North Mankato, Minnesota 56003
www.capstonepub.com

Library of Congress Cataloging-in-Publication Data
Names: Toth, Henrietta, author.
Title: Lil Nas X : record-breaking musician who blurs the lines / by
   Henrietta Toth.
Description: North Mankato : Capstone Press, 2021. | Series: Movers,
   shakers, and history makers | Includes index.
Identifiers: LCCN 2020000946 (print) | LCCN 2020000947 (ebook) | ISBN
   9781496684813 (hardcover) | ISBN 9781496688231 (paperback) | ISBN
   9781496685018 (pdf)
Subjects: LCSH: Lil Nas X, 1999—Juvenile literature. | Rap
   musicians—United States—Biography—Juvenile literature.
Classification: LCC ML3930.L465 T67 2021 (print) | LCC ML3930.L465
   (ebook) | DDC 782.421649092 [B]—dc23
LC record available at https://lccn.loc.gov/2020000946
LC ebook record available at https://lccn.loc.gov/2020000947

Image Credits
AP Images: mpi04/MediaPunch/Ipx, cover (foreground); Getty Images: Kevin Mazur/Getty Images Entertainment, 36, Mike Coppola/MTV/Getty Images Entertainment, 25; iStockphoto: Circle Creative Studio, 33, rodclementphotography, 6; Red Line Editorial: 10; Rex Features: AFF-USA/Shutterstock, 19, Charles Sykes/Invision/AP/Shutterstock, 43, Chelsea Lauren/Shutterstock, 13, David Fisher/Shutterstock, 30, Matt Baron/Shutterstock, 35, Rob Latour/Shutterstock, 15, 22, 40, Scott Roth/Invision/AP/Shutterstock, 39, Stephen Lovekin/Shutterstock, 5; Shutterstock Images: Chaay_Tee, 9, Derrek Kupish, 29, Ververidis Vasilis, cover (background), 1, XanderSt, 17

Editorial Credits
Editor: Charly Haley; Designer: Colleen McLaren; Production Specialist: Ryan Gale

Printed in the United States of America.
PA117

CONTENTS

Words in **bold** are in the glossary.

CHAPTER ONE

THE EARLY YEARS

A young rapper took the internet by storm with a cowboy **persona** and the song "Old Town Road." This is how Lil Nas X launched his music career in 2019. His song "Old Town Road" was one of the most successful songs of that year. It spent a record 19 weeks on the *Billboard* Hot 100 Chart, which tracks the songs that people are listening to and buying the most. The song has a country melody with booming hip-hop beats. This mix of **genres** caught a lot of attention. With "Old Town Road," it seemed like Lil Nas X's career was born overnight. It was a dream come true for the young artist from Georgia.

GROWING UP IN GEORGIA

Lil Nas X was born on April 9, 1999, in Atlanta, Georgia. Today everyone knows him as Lil Nas X, but his birth name was Montero Lamar Hill.

Lil Nas X often dresses like a cowboy as part of his well-known persona.

Lil Nas X lived in Atlanta until he was 9 years old.

Lil Nas X has five older siblings. His parents divorced when he was 6 years old. For a few years, Lil Nas X lived with his mother and grandmother. They lived in a **public housing** project in Atlanta. It wasn't very safe. It could be dangerous. Sometimes crimes happened. People used drugs there.

At age 9, Lil Nas X and his brother moved in with their father and stepmother. They lived in a suburb of Atlanta. Later the family moved to a small city about thirty minutes away.

AN INTERNET STAR

Lil Nas X says he was a class clown, but he was also serious about school. However, he was most interested in music. In fourth grade, he learned to play the trumpet. He played it until high school. He also listened to hip-hop.

By high school, Lil Nas X started spending more time on the internet than hanging out with friends. He was searching for something creative to do online. He wanted to make a name for himself. He looked for ways to create a persona and get followers. And he wanted to figure out how to make money from internet fame.

Lil Nas X posted to Facebook and Instagram. He made videos for Vine and YouTube. Then he found that he liked posting funny tweets to Twitter. That was where he started to go viral.

WHAT IS TIKTOK?

TikTok is a popular social media app that launched in 2017. More than 500 million users post creative videos on TikTok. Many share videos of themselves singing and dancing. Some, like Lil Nas X, have so many fans that they've become famous on TikTok and beyond.

Before he became a famous musician, Lil Nas X grew his fanbase on social media.

Some of Lil Nas X's jokes were retweeted thousands of times. Many people believe he got this attention on Twitter by "tweetdecking." Tweetdecking was a way to use an app to inflate the number of tweets across several accounts.

Some tweetdeckers used stolen tweets. Tweetdecking has been banned because it violated Twitter's spam policy. Lil Nas X has never admitted to being a tweetdecker.

Lil Nas X had a lot of followers by 2015. He made popular memes and Twitter threads about pop culture. Then Lil Nas X started posting to TikTok. That's where his song "Old Town Road" eventually went viral.

CHAPTER TWO

MAKING MUSIC

Lil Nas X graduated from high school in 2017. That fall he began classes at the University of West Georgia. He studied computer science because he wanted to invent an app. Instead, he ended up spending much of his time making music.

Lil Nas X started writing songs the summer after his first year of college. It was difficult for him at first. But by his fifth song, he was remixing music to create new versions of one song. He found beats on YouTube and rapped to them. Around this time, he started using the name Lil Nas X. He posted his first song online in May 2018. It was called "Shame." By late July, he added a **mixtape** called *Nasarati*.

When Lil Nas X first began writing songs, he could only dream about the fame that he has today.

13

Lil Nas X decided not to go back to college in the fall. "I was doing good in school, but I didn't want to do school anymore," he said. He got jobs at the fast-food chain Zaxby's and at the Six Flags Over Georgia theme park. He wanted to make music on the internet, and he thought he could create a career out of it. He lived with a sister, slept on her floor, and spent a lot of time on the internet. He tried out different versions of songs and posted them online.

WHY THE NAME LIL NAS X?

Lil Nas X first used the name *Nas* on social media. Nas is also the name of another famous rapper from the 1990s. Lil Nas X added the *Lil* to describe himself as a new rapper. The *X* is the Roman numeral for 10. That's how many years Lil Nas X thought it would take for him to become a legendary music star.

In 2020, the rapper Nas (left), who inspired Lil Nas X's stage name, joined Lil Nas X on a remix of the younger rapper's song "Rodeo."

At first, his songs were hardly noticed. But Lil Nas X used social media to promote himself. He started to get a lot of followers. Lil Nas X was on his way to building his music career.

CHAPTER THREE

A HIT SONG

Lil Nas X did not start his music career in the usual way. Typically record labels seek out talented artists and offer them recording contracts. Record labels help artists get their music out to big audiences. Instead, Lil Nas X turned to the internet to create a hit song.

For his breakout hit "Old Town Road," Lil Nas X found a beat online and bought it for $30 from a Dutch song producer. The beat sampled a song by the rock band Nine Inch Nails. Lil Nas X worked with the beat and combined country and hip-hop music. This mix of genres is called country rap. Then Lil Nas X added catchy lyrics. He says the words are about leaving his old life for a new life and career.

Lil Nas X used TikTok to help make "Old Town Road" go viral.

On December 3, 2018, Lil Nas X released "Old Town Road" online. He posted it to TikTok a couple of months later. People loved his cowboy rapper persona. Fans posted clips of themselves in cowboy gear dancing to "Old Town Road." Radio DJs took the song from YouTube to play it on the air.

ON THE CHARTS

By March 2019, "Old Town Road" had made it onto three *Billboard* charts: Hot 100, Hot Country Songs, and Hot R&B/Hip-Hop Songs. The song spent one week on the Hot Country Songs chart before *Billboard* removed it. Many people said this move was racist. They believed that "Old Town Road" was pulled off the country chart because Lil Nas X is black, when many country artists are white.

FACT

While Lil Nas X was writing the lyrics to "Old Town Road," he thought about how he could share the song through memes.

Even Lil Nas X felt something wasn't right. "You can have your country song with [hip-hop] elements, but if it's by known country artists, then it's allowed," he said. "A black guy who raps comes along, and he's on top of the country chart, it's like, 'What . . . ?'" But *Billboard* denied any racism, saying "Old Town Road" was a hip-hop and pop song and was misclassified as country.

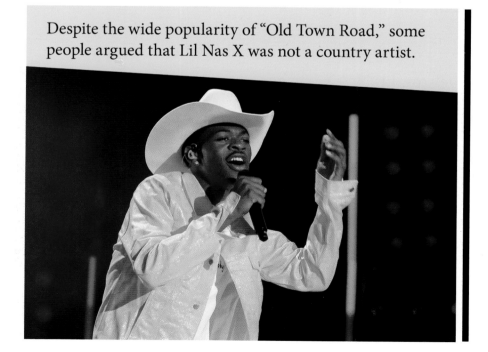

Despite the wide popularity of "Old Town Road," some people argued that Lil Nas X was not a country artist.

THE REMIX

Not long after that, Lil Nas X released a remix of "Old Town Road" with country music star Billy Ray Cyrus. The video of "Old Town Road" features Lil Nas X and Cyrus dressed like cowboys. It has **cameos** by other celebrities, including comedian Chris Rock. Lil Nas X likes to work with other people. The remix of "Old Town Road" made the song even more popular.

"Old Town Road" has inspired other remixes and videos too. Country singer Keith Urban recorded a **cover** of the song.

With these remixes and his blending of music genres, Lil Nas X has become known as someone who can't fit one category. He blended the genres of country and rap for "Old Town Road." He works with different musicians, comedians, and others. People might expect a musician to just do one thing, but Lil Nas X mixes it up.

THE "OLD TOWN ROAD" CREW

Lil Nas X had a lot of people in his "Old Town Road" video with Billy Ray Cyrus. Other people in the music video include:

- CHRIS ROCK, COMEDIAN
- DIPLO, DJ AND MUSIC PRODUCER
- HAHA DAVIS, COMEDIAN AND YOUTUBER
- RICO NASTY, RAPPER
- VINCE STAPLES, RAPPER
- YOUNGKIO, MUSIC PRODUCER

BREAKING A RECORD

"Old Town Road" reached the top of the *Billboard* Hot 100 chart on April 9, 2019. That was also Lil Nas X's 20th birthday. "Old Town Road" stayed at the top spot for 19 weeks. This was an all-time record.

Billy Ray Cyrus (left) and Lil Nas X perform "Old Town Road" at the 2020 Grammy Awards.

FACT

Before the "Old Town Road" remix, Billy Ray Cyrus's biggest song was "Achy Breaky Heart." It reached number four on the *Billboard* Hot 100 in 1992.

By July, "Old Town Road" had more than 70 million streams. It had become the fastest-selling song in the country. By August, he had earned between $3 million and $4 million. By October, the song had sold more than 10 million copies. That made it diamond certified. "Old Town Road" had launched Lil Nas X's career.

CHAPTER FOUR

RISE TO FAME

"Old Town Road" took Lil Nas X from internet stardom to mainstream fame. In March 2019, he signed with Columbia Records. The record label helped him produce his first **EP**.

Lil Nas X soon released his EP called 7. It has eight songs, including the original and remix versions of "Old Town Road."

The song "Panini" off of the EP was released as a single. It's not country rap like "Old Town Road," and it's not about a panini sandwich. It's based on a character from the cartoon TV show *Chowder*. The song peaked at No. 5 on the *Billboard* Hot 100 and reached the top of the YouTube chart.

Lil Nas X performed the song "Panini," from the EP 7, at the MTV Video Music Awards in 2019.

MUSIC RELEASES BY LIL NAS X

MAY 2018: The song "Shame" is released online.

JULY 2018: The *Nasarati* mixtape is released online.

DECEMBER 2018: "Old Town Road" is released online.

APRIL 2019: The "Old Town Road" remix with Billy Ray Cyrus is released through Columbia Records.

JUNE 2019: The *7* EP is released.

JUNE 2019: The single "Panini" is released.

At the height of this success, Lil Nas X made a big personal announcement. He came out as gay at the end of June 2019. Though some fans didn't like this, many supported Lil Nas X. Meanwhile, "Old Town Road" remained at the top of the charts and would soon earn many awards.

AWARDS

In November 2019, Lil Nas X made music history by becoming the first gay black artist to win a Country Music Award. He and Billy Ray Cyrus shared the award for Vocal Event of the Year for "Old Town Road."

It was one of many awards they would soon win. Lil Nas X also won the BET Hip-Hop Award for Best Single of the Year in 2019. He and Cyrus shared a BET Hip-Hop Award for Best Collab/Duo or Group. Lil Nas X also won the MTV Video Music Award for Song of the Year. He shared the Teen Choice Award for Choice R&B/Hip-Hop Song with Cyrus.

Lil Nas X was nominated for five American Music Awards and won Favorite Song-Rap/Hip-Hop with Cyrus. The Grammy Awards are considered the most prestigious in music. Lil Nas X was nominated six times. He and Cyrus shared the awards for Best Pop Duo/Group Performance and Best Music Video.

Lil Nas X has been on several national TV shows to perform songs and be interviewed. This includes *CBS This Morning* and *The Ellen DeGeneres Show*.

THE CRITICS

Fame has had some downsides for Lil Nas X. Some music **critics** have been hard on him. They have panned 7 and "Old Town Road." Critics have said Lil Nas X is more focused on getting his music online than on the sound of it.

But Lil Nas X doesn't care about these critics. He points out that "Old Town Road" was the number one song in the country.

Cyrus (left) and Lil Nas X sat together at the 2019 Country Music Awards.

Lil Nas X holds up his Grammy awards. In addition to accepting his Grammys, he performed at the awards show with several other artists.

In "Old Town Road," Lil Nas X mentions Wrangler jeans with the verse, "Wrangler on my booty." This inspired the clothing company to partner with Lil Nas X to make a limited fashion line.

"OLD TOWN ROAD" REMIXES

Lil Nas X and Billy Ray Cyrus's "Old Town Road" remix was a huge hit. But Lil Nas X has remixed the track with other artists too, including:

- # DIPLO
- # YOUNG THUG AND MASON
- # RM OF BTS

Fans can buy T-shirts with Lil Nas X's name. They can also buy blue jeans with "Wrangler" printed on the backside, as in Lil Nas X's lyric.

But the Lil Nas X Collection was criticized by some Wrangler customers. These customers claimed that "Old Town Road" doesn't really represent cowboys or country music. Lil Nas X tweeted that he was surprised by the **backlash**. Other people have said the backlash is a result of racism.

CHAPTER FIVE

COMING OUT

Coming out was a big decision for Lil Nas X. But he said it felt right. As a young boy, Lil Nas X knew he was gay, but he didn't think it was ok. He prayed it was a phase of growing up. By his mid-teens, Lil Nas X came to accept his gay identity.

He didn't know how his family and fans would react to the news. First, he told his father and one of his sisters. He says this was difficult to do. But then he wanted to tell his fans. He dropped hints on Twitter asking his fans to pay attention to the lyrics of his song "C7osure." Then he tweeted the cover art of his EP with its rainbow colors.

Lil Nas X said Pride Month celebrations encouraged him to come out.

Part of the reason Lil Nas X came out publicly in June was because June is LGBTQ Pride Month. "I never would have done that if I wasn't in a way pushed by the universe. In June, I'm seeing Pride flags everywhere and seeing couples holding hands—little stuff like that," he said.

BACKLASH AND SUPPORT

Lil Nas X expected some backlash to his coming out because there aren't many openly gay country or hip-hop stars. But after he came out, "Old Town Road" stayed at the top of the *Billboard* Hot 100.

LGBTQ PRIDE MONTH

LGBTQ stands for lesbian, gay, bisexual, transgender, and queer. People celebrate LGBTQ rights in June. The celebration is called Pride Month. It also remembers the Stonewall riots of 1969, when police raided a gay bar in New York City and were met with resistance. Gay pride parades are held in many cities across the world. The celebrations encouraged Lil Nas X to come out in June 2019.

Despite backlash and criticism, Lil Nas X stays true to himself.

Lil Nas X received support from Miley Cyrus (left) and other celebrities after he came out.

Some Lil Nas X fans saw his announcement as a publicity stunt. Some people posted negative comments on his Instagram. But many fans supported Lil Nas X. Other celebrities, such as Cardi B and Miley Cyrus, who is Billy Ray Cyrus's daughter, supported him too. They praised him for coming out during Pride Month and while he's so popular.

Lil Nas X says his fame has helped him embrace who he is. He hopes he can help pave the way for other young LGBTQ people to do the same.

CHAPTER SIX

WHAT'S NEXT?

Lil Nas X has created his own path to a big music career. He says he has a 10-year plan to continue making great music.

For Lil Nas X, making more music means experimenting with new sounds and different genres. He looks forward to more collaborations. He's also eager for his fans to see how his music grows.

Music is important to Lil Nas X. But after having such a busy and successful year in 2019, he said it might be time for a vacation. Yet he's afraid that if he stays away from music too long, his fans might stop caring about him.

Lil Nas X took time to buy an apartment in Los Angeles, California, in June 2019. He has said he might buy a house or land in Atlanta someday.

Lil Nas X plans to continue writing and experimenting with music.

Lil Nas X performs with the group BTS at the 2020 Grammy Awards.

Lil Nas X may eventually change his name from Nas because of the other rapper named Nas. Lil Nas X explained in a tweet, "Nas is a legend and I never meant any disrespect by my stage name."

MAKING A DIFFERENCE

Lil Nas X hopes to use his fame to make a difference. He has found time to fit good deeds into his busy career. In May 2019, he surprised the students at Lander Elementary School in Mayfield Heights, Ohio, with a concert. He performed "Old Town Road" for them after he had seen a viral video of the students dancing to the song.

WHO IS NAS?

Nas is a rapper from New York City. He was born in 1973. His first album, *Illmatic*, greatly influenced hip-hop music in the 1990s. Nas has been nominated for 13 Grammy awards.

Lil Nas X also performed at his old high school in Georgia in September 2019. Later that month, he visited an 11-year-old fan who was a patient at a children's hospital in Atlanta.

Lil Nas X's songs have made a huge difference for some fans. A mother tweeted that her young autistic son who didn't speak began humming the tune to "Old Town Road." Then he started singing the words. Lil Nas X tweeted his reaction to the news and called the boy a king.

Lil Nas X believes he's making the biggest difference with his brand of music and the viral way he promotes it. He says, "Kids are going to grow up with that song and play it to remember these times, which makes me feel amazing."

Fans are excited to see what Lil Nas X does next.

TIMELINE

1999: Lil Nas X is born as Montero Lamar Hill on April 9.

2015: Lil Nas X develops an internet presence on Facebook, Instagram, and Twitter.

2017: Lil Nas X graduates from high school and attends the University of West Georgia for one year.

2018: Lil Nas X joins YouTube.

2018: Lil Nas X drops out of college.

2018: Lil Nas X begins writing songs. He posts his first song and EP online.

2018: Lil Nas X releases the country rap song "Old Town Road."

2019: "Old Town Road" makes the *Billboard* Hot 100.

2019: Lil Nas X makes a remix of "Old Town Road" with Billy Ray Cyrus. The song reaches the top of the *Billboard* Hot 100 and stays there for a record 19 weeks.

2019: Lil Nas X releases the EP *7*.

2019: Lil Nas X comes out as gay.

2019: "Old Town Road" becomes diamond certified, selling more than 10 million copies.

2020: Lil Nas X wins two Grammy awards.

GLOSSARY

backlash (BAK-lash)
a strong negative reaction

cameo (KA-me-yoh)
a brief appearance by a
celebrity in a music video,
movie, or TV show

cover (KUH-ver)
a version of a well-known
song made by a different
artist

critics (KRIT-iks)
people who tell the good
and bad of something

EP (EE PEE)
short for extended play,
a music release that has
fewer songs than a full
album

genres (ZHAHN-ruhs)
styles or types of music

mixtape (miks-TAYP)
a collection of songs that
is usually less organized
and lower quality than an
album

persona (per-SOHN-uh)
a person's character
or role as presented to
others

**public housing
(pub-LIK HOW-zing)**
government-owned
housing for low-income
families

READ MORE

Duncan, Terri Kaye. *Cardi B: Rapper and Online Star*. New York: Enslow Publishing, 2020.

Hudalla, Jamie. *Chance the Rapper: Independent Master of Hip-Hop Flow*. North Mankato, MN: Capstone Press, 2021.

Morse, Eric. *What Is Hip-Hop?* New York: Akashic Books, 2017.

INTERNET SITES

Billboard **Hot 100**
www.billboard.com/charts/hot-100

Lil Nas X Official Website
www.lilnasx.com

Lil Nas X on Instagram
www.instagram.com/lilnasx

INDEX

Quote Sources
p. 14, "I was doing good…" Lakin Starling, "Lil Nas X Talks Fame, Going Viral, and More in His First Cover Story," *Teen Vogue*, June 3, 2019, https://www.teenvogue.com/story/lil-nas-x-june-2019-cover Accessed 13 March 2020.
p. 19, "You can have your…" Ibid., Accessed 13 March 2020.
p. 34, "I never would have…" Andrew R. Chow, "It Feels Like I'm Chosen to Do This: Inside the Record-Breaking Rise of Lil Nas X," *Time*, August 15, 2019, https://time.com/magazine/us/5652772/august-26th-2019-vol-194-no-7-u-s/ Accessed 13 March 2020.
p. 41, "Nas is a legend…" Carl Lamarre, "Lil Nas X Is Considering Changing His Stage Name Out of Respect for Nas," *Billboard*, April 25, 2019, https://www.billboard.com/articles/columns/hip-hop/8508726/lil-nas-x-nas-name-change Accessed 13 March 2020.
p. 42, "Kids are going to…" Al Horner, "Lil Nas X: 'I'm Still in the First Stage of Figuring Out Who I Am,'" *GQ*, August 5, 2019, https://www.gq-magazine.co.uk/culture/article/lil-nas-x-interview Accessed 13 March 2020.